Super Simple
CHINESE ART

Fun and Easy Art from Around the World

Alex Kuskowski

Consulting Editor, Diane Craig, M.A./Reading Specialist

A Division of ABDO

ABDO
Publishing Company

visit us at www.abdopublishing.com

Published by ABDO Publishing Company, a division of ABDO, P.O. Box 398166, Minneapolis, Minnesota 55439. Copyright © 2012 by Abdo Consulting Group, Inc. International copyrights reserved in all countries. No part of this book may be reproduced in any form without written permission from the publisher. Super SandCastle™ is a trademark and logo of ABDO Publishing Company.

Printed in the United States of America, North Mankato, Minnesota
102011
012012

Editor: Liz Salzmann
Content Developer: Nancy Tuminelly
Interior Design and Production: Oona Gaarder-Juntti, Mighty Media, Inc.
Cover Design: Kelsey Gullickson, Mighty Media, Inc.
Photo Credits: Jupiterimages, Shutterstock, Thinkstock

The following manufacturers/names appearing in this book are trademarks:
Elmer's®, Elmer's® Glue-All™, Fiskars®, Glitter Glue™, Scotch®

Library of Congress Cataloging-in-Publication Data
Kuskowski, Alex.
  Super simple Chinese art : fun and easy art from around the world / Alex Kuskowski.
      p. cm. -- (Super simple cultural art)
  ISBN 978-1-61783-212-3
  1. Handicraft--Juvenile literature. 2. China--Civilization--Miscellanea--Juvenile literature. I. Title.
  TT160.K874 2012
  745.5--dc23
                            2011024602

Super SandCastle™ books are created by a team of professional educators, reading specialists, and content developers around five essential components—phonemic awareness, phonics, vocabulary, text comprehension, and fluency—to assist young readers as they develop reading skills and strategies and increase their general knowledge. All books are written, reviewed, and leveled for guided reading, early reading intervention, and Accelerated Reader® programs for use in shared, guided, and independent reading and writing activities to support a balanced approach to literacy instruction.

TO ADULT HELPERS

Children can have a lot of fun learning about different cultures through arts and crafts. Be sure to supervise them as they work on the projects in this book. Let the kids do as much as possible on their own. But be ready to step in and help if necessary. Also, kids may be using glue, paint, markers, and clay. Make sure they protect their clothes and work surfaces.

Symbol

ADULT HELPER
Ask for help. You will need help from an adult.

Table of Contents

Chinese Plum Blossom

The Chinese plum tree blooms in the winter. The flowers stand for courage and hope.

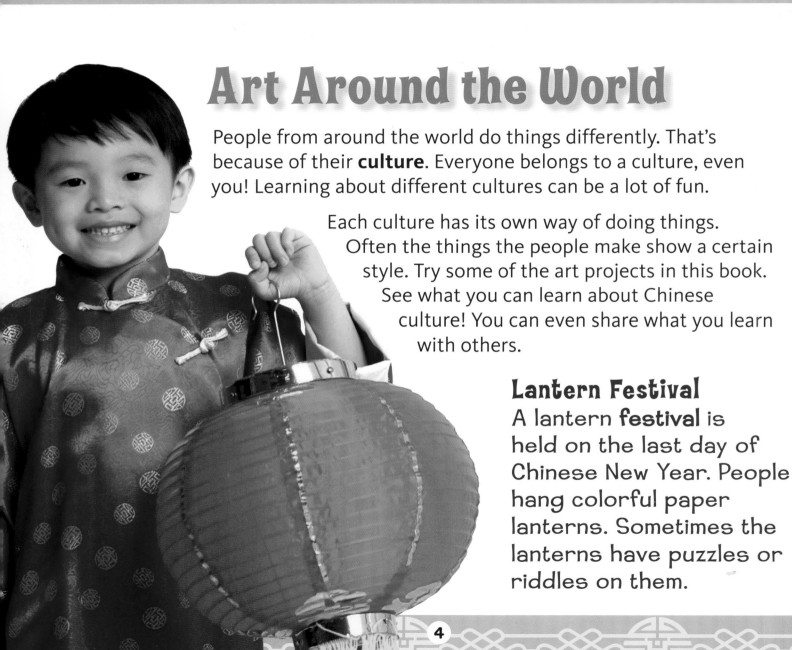

Art Around the World

People from around the world do things differently. That's because of their **culture**. Everyone belongs to a culture, even you! Learning about different cultures can be a lot of fun.

Each culture has its own way of doing things. Often the things the people make show a certain style. Try some of the art projects in this book. See what you can learn about Chinese culture! You can even share what you learn with others.

Lantern Festival

A lantern **festival** is held on the last day of Chinese New Year. People hang colorful paper lanterns. Sometimes the lanterns have puzzles or riddles on them.

Before You Start

Remember to treat other people and **cultures** with respect. Respect their art, **jewelry**, and clothes too. These things can have special meaning to people.

There are a few rules for doing art projects.

- **Permission**

  Make sure to ask permission to do a project. You might want to use things you find around the house. Ask first!

- **Safety**

  Get help from an adult when using something hot or sharp. Never use an oven by yourself.

Chinese Dragon

Chinese dragons stand for strength and good luck. Many people make giant dragon puppets. They do dragon dances during Chinese New Year parades.

Art in the Chinese Culture

People in China create many beautiful things. Some are for everyday use. Others are for special occasions. The **designs** in Chinese art often have special meanings.

Rattle-Drum

The first rattle-drums were made more than 2,000 years ago. Rattle-drums are used in music and at parties. They are also popular toys for children.

Giant Panda

China is the only place giant pandas live in the wild. The giant panda is a **symbol** of peace and friendship.

Fireworks

Fireworks were invented in China more than 1,000 years ago. The loud bangs were thought to scare away bad spirits. Today, fireworks are used at many parties and holidays.

Lion Dance

Two people wear a lion costume for a lion dance. It is performed during holidays such as Chinese New Year. It is thought to bring good luck and protect people from bad spirits.

Materials

Here are some of the materials you'll need to get started.

pencil

unsharpened pencil

tape

glitter glue

markers

paintbrushes

hole punch

construction paper

glue stick

acrylic paint

brown chenille stems

ruler

scissors

chopsticks

stapler

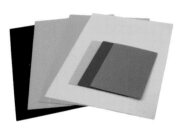
craft foam

8

glue

wooden dowels

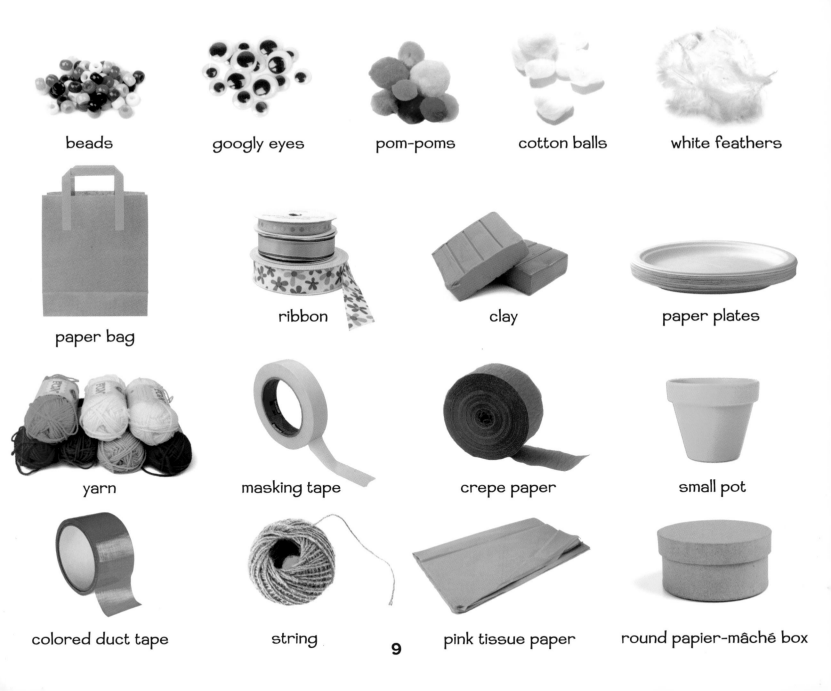

beads

googly eyes

pom-poms

cotton balls

white feathers

paper bag

ribbon

clay

paper plates

yarn

masking tape

crepe paper

small pot

colored duct tape

string

9

pink tissue paper

round papier-mâché box

PLUM BLOSSOM TREE

Make these pretty flowers to brighten up your winter days!

WHAT YOU NEED
- small pot
- acrylic paint
- paintbrush
- clay
- 6 brown chenille stems
- scissors
- pink tissue paper
- ruler
- glue

1. Paint the pot. Let the paint dry. Put a small amount of clay in the bottom of the pot.

2. Cut the chenille stems into pieces. Make the pieces different sizes. Twist shorter ones onto longer ones. Make them look like tree branches. Stick the branches into the clay in the pot.

3. Cut the tissue paper into squares. The sides should be about 1 to 2 inches (2 to 5 cm) long. Pinch the middle of each square and twist the paper. Try to make it look like a tiny flower.

4. Put dots of glue on the ends of the branches. Press a tissue paper flower to each drop of glue. Let the glue dry.

SPINNING RATTLE-DRUM

Make a rattle-drum and spin it to your own beat.

1. Remove the lid from the papier-mâché box. Paint the outside of the box and the lid red. Paint pictures or **designs** on the top and bottom. Let the paint dry.

2. Punch a hole in the side of the box. It should be big enough for the wooden dowel to fit through. Make sure the lid won't cover the hole.

3. Stick the wooden dowel through the hole. Put glue on the end of the dowel. Press it against the other side of the box. Let the glue dry.

4. Punch a hole on one side of the box. It should be even with the center of the dowel.

5 Cut an 8-inch (20 cm) ribbon. Tie a knot in one end. Push the other end of the ribbon through the hole from the inside.

6 Tape the knot to the inside of the box.

7 Put two beads on the ribbon. Tie a knot in the end. Push the beads against the knot. Tie a knot on the other side of the beads.

8 Repeat steps 4 through 7 on the other side of the box. Put glue around the inside of the lid. Put the lid on the box. Let the glue dry.

9 Hold the dowel and turn the drum back and forth. The beads will hit the sides of the drum!

14

FiREWORK Fan

Make your own fun fireworks that will last all year!

WHAT YOU NEED
- construction paper
- glitter glue
- ruler
- glue stick
- duct tape
- scissors
- chopsticks

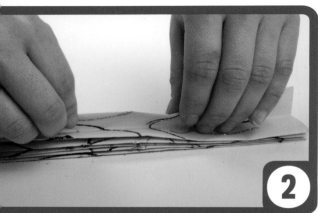

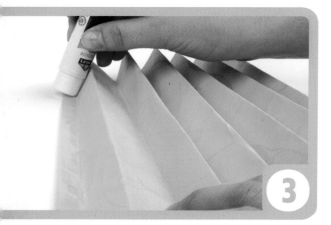

1 Choose six sheets of construction paper that are the same color. Decorate each sheet with glitter glue. Make colorful swirls and **designs**! Let the glue dry.

2 Fold the short side of one sheet ½ inch (2 cm). Turn the paper over and fold it again. Keep folding back and forth until the whole sheet is folded. Fold all of the sheets of paper this way.

3 Put glue along the edge of one of the sheets. Press the end of another sheet onto the glued edge.

4 Repeat step 3 until all the sheets are glued together. It should be one long sheet.

5 Push all the folds together into a **stack**. Cut off a piece of duct tape. Tape one end of the paper stack together. Make sure it's taped tightly. Use more tape if necessary.

6 Glue a chopstick to each side of the stack. The ends should stick out about 3 inches (8 cm) past the untaped end of the paper stack. Let the glue dry.

7 Carefully pull the chopsticks apart to open the fan. Bring the sticks all the way around until they meet. Hold the fan by the sticks.

HANGING LANTERN

This paper lantern makes a great party decoration!

18

1. Cut three sheets of construction paper in half crosswise.

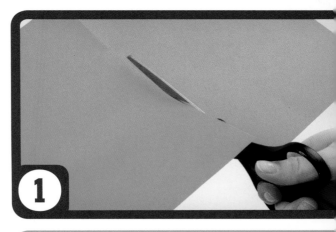

2. Decorate the construction paper. Use paint or glitter glue. You could draw flower **designs** or Chinese **symbols**. Let the paint or glue dry.

3. Lay each sheet down with the designs facing up. Fold the long sides of each sheet up about ¼ inch (.5 cm).

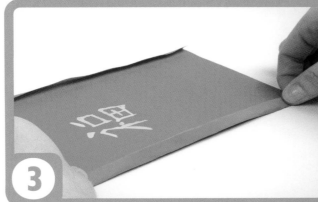

4. Glue the sheets together at the folded edges. It will make a hexagon shape. The designs should face out.

5. Punch a hole in the top of one sheet. Then punch a hole directly across from the first hole.

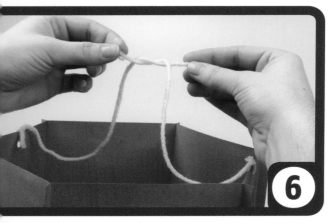

6 Cut two pieces of yarn 12 inches (30 cm) long. Tie one to each hole. Tie the two pieces together

7 Cut five pieces of yarn 10 inches (25 cm) long. Group them together and fold them in half.

8 Cut an 8-inch (20 cm) piece of yarn. Wrap it around the folded yarn about 1 inch (3 cm) below the fold. Wrap it several times. Then tie a knot. Now you have a tassel.

9 Cut a 6-inch (15 cm) piece of yarn. Tie it to the **loop** in the tassel. Punch a hole in the bottom of the lantern. Tie the tassel to the lantern.

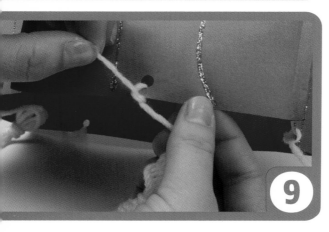

10 Repeat steps 7 through 9 to make as many tassels as you want.

20

Lion Mask

Make up a lion dance to go with your new lion mask.

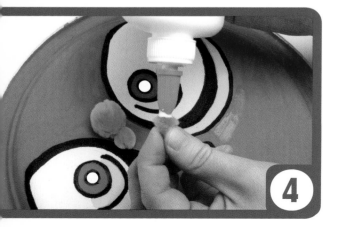

1 Draw the lion's eyes and nose on a paper plate.

2 Have an adult help you cut out holes for your eyes.

3 Paint the plate with red, yellow, and green paint. Let the paint dry. Trace over the black lines with the marker.

4 Glue pom-poms to the nose and forehead.

22

5. Pull apart white cotton balls. Glue the fluffy cotton around the eyes and mouth.

6. Glue white feathers over the cotton balls.

7. Cut the mouth out of red foam. Cut teeth out of white foam. Glue the teeth to the mouth. Glue the mouth to the mask.

8. Cut some strips of crepe paper. Tape them to the bottom of the mask.

9. Punch a hole on both sides of the mask. Tie a piece of yarn to each hole. Tie the yarn together to wear your mask.

BREEZY Kite

Kites were invented in China almost 3,000 years ago!

1. Cut along one side of the paper bag. Cut off the bottom of the bag.

2. Open the bag. Measure a rectangle 12 by 16 inches (30 by 41 cm). Cut out the rectangle.

3. Fold the rectangle in half crosswise. Lay it down with the folded side on the left. Measure 4 inches (10 cm) in from the right side. Mark it on the top edge. Measure 4 inches (10 cm) in from the right side again. Mark it on the bottom edge.

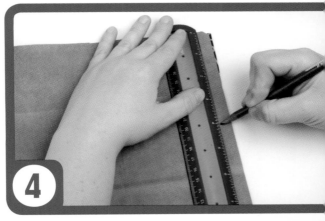

4. Measure 4 inches (10 cm) down from the top. Mark it on the right edge.

5. Use the ruler to draw a line from the top mark to the side mark. Then draw a line from the bottom mark to the side mark.

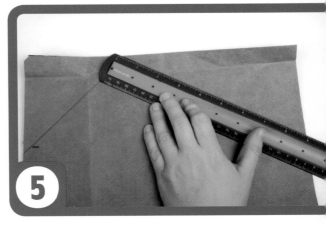

6 Cut along the lines. Make sure you cut through both layers. Open up the kite. Decorate it using paint or markers.

7 Fold the sides of the kite in toward the center. Rub the folds to make sharp **creases**.

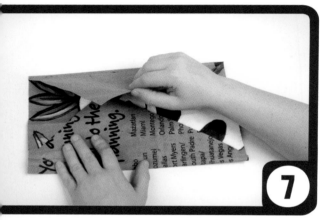

8 Open the sides. Tape a chopstick in the middle of each crease.

9 Cut three long pieces of crepe paper. Staple them to the bottom of the kite. Space them out evenly.

26

10. Fold a piece of tape over each side corner. Punch a hole through the tape on each side.

11. Cut two pieces of string 16 inches (41 cm) long. Tie one to each hole. Then tie the ends together.

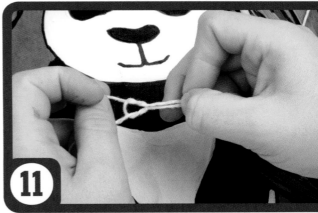

12. Cut a piece of string about 50 feet (15 m) long. Tie one end to an unsharpened pencil. Wrap the string around the pencil. Tie the other end to the strings on the kite. Tie it where the strings are knotted together.

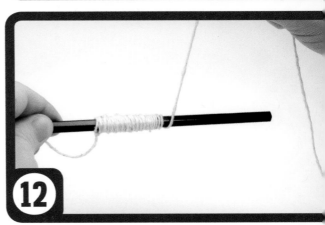

27

LUCKY RED ENVELOPE

Gifts of money are often put in red envelopes for good luck.

1. Draw a line across the foam lengthwise. It should be 1 inch (3 cm) from one edge. Draw two lines from this line to the edge. They should be 3 inches (8 cm) from each side. Cut off the left and right rectangles.

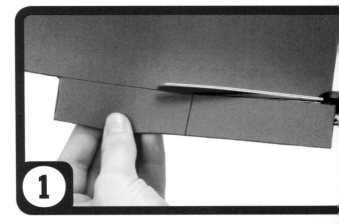

2. Fold one side over 3 inches (8 cm). Put glue on the back of the fold. Fold the other side over on top of the glue.

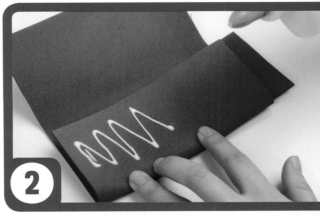

3. Put glue on the flap. Fold it on top of the folded sides.

4. Draw a good luck sign on the **envelope**. Use glitter glue so it shines. Let the glue dry.

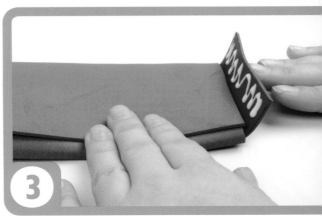

5. Make fake money out of construction paper. Put it in the envelope!

GREEN DRAGON PUPPET

Have a dragon puppet parade with your friends!

1 Cut a dragon head out of green craft foam. Glue on googly eyes and foam shapes. Don't forget the flames! Cut a tail out of green craft foam. Decorate the tail with glitter glue.

2 Cut a piece of construction paper 3 by 15 inches (8 by 38 cm). Fold the short side of the paper 1 inch (3 cm). Turn it over and fold it again. Fold back and forth until the whole paper is folded. This is the dragon's body.

3 Decorate the body. Make **designs** with glitter glue. Glue on short pieces of ribbon. Glue the head to one end of the body. Glue the tail to the other end.

4 Glue one chopstick behind the head. Glue the other chopstick behind the tail.

31

Conclusion

Did you learn about Chinese **culture**? Did you have fun making these art projects? Learning about other cultures is very interesting. You can learn about how people around the world live. Try looking up more **information** about Chinese people!

Glossary

crease – a line made by folding something.

culture – the ideas, traditions, art, and behaviors of a group of people.

design – a decorative pattern or arrangement.

envelope – a container for something flat, such as a letter.

festival – a celebration that happens at the same time each year.

information – the facts known about an event or subject.

jewelry – pretty things, such as rings, necklaces, and bracelets, that you wear for decoration.

loop – a circle made by a rope, string, or thread.

stack – a pile of things placed one on top of the other.

symbol – an object or picture that stands for or represents something.